BUG-OUT BAG BASICS

M. SHAWN WHITLEY

ISBN-13: 978-1482756593
ISBN-10: 1482756595

Printed in the United States of America.

Thanks to Jill and Julie,
for helping make this happen.

Contents

INTRODUCTION

It is more important now than ever to be prepared. As technology advances and people become a society of "buy it now" or "get on demand," we have come to expect the same of our government. Unfortunately, this expectation is totally unrealistic during any type of incident or natural disaster. That statement is not to take away from any government establishments whose purpose is to provide relief after such events, only to say that when we need them to respond, it won't happen at the click of a button. It takes time to identify what the needs are, time to gather resources, time to respond to the incident, and time to implement the strategy and tactics to accomplish the mission. All of that just does not happen instantly and never will, no matter how advanced technology and training become.

I have been an emergency responder since 2004 and have had the opportunity to respond to numerous small and large incidents, some of which include Hurricanes Katrina, Ike and Sandy and catastrophic wildfires in Texas and Georgia (these being the larger fire incidents in my career). A perception that I have gained over the years is how unprepared the general public is and how they expect the government to fix the issue without assuming any responsibility or ownership of their situation.

If you don't pack up your belongings and evacuate before a hurricane makes landfall, when there is still time, why should you get to point your finger at the government and place blame because "it took too long for them to get here"? It is each person's responsibility to take care of himself and his family. If an incident occurs on such a large scale that support systems are wiped out, are you going to be tapping your foot on the front porch and watching the seconds pass on your watch, waiting for assistance?

Realistically, you need to provide for yourself for at least the first 72 hours after the initial incident has occurred. More likely than not, responding agencies will have begun recovery efforts by this time; however, both the size of the area affected and the magnitude of the incident can delay those efforts.

So what am I getting at? *Be prepared*. The stocking of extra food and water is a wonderful idea, but what if you have to leave your home? What if your home is damaged or destroyed? The best preparation that an individual can do to equip himself for any disaster is simply to build a bug-out bag.

A *what*?

A bug-out bag.

In this book, I'm going to list and explain items to put in your bag. Tips on packing, insulation, periodic inventory, and inspection will also be covered. Many of the items listed are what I use during deployment to disasters and what I have in my own personal bug-out bag. Building a bag is very simple, and this book will deliver a simple message. I am not trying to make my book get on the best sellers list or seeking any kind of publicity. What I am trying to do is get you ready before the next disaster strikes. So in this book, you will not find dramatic photos and flashy quotes—just the bare-bones information.

The process of building a bug-out bag is really quite simple, and not everything has to be purchased at once. You can pull from some items you already have around your home. However, I do very sternly warn against taking items out of your bug-out bag and using them when it isn't a time of disaster. What happens if you use it, promise yourself that you'll replace it tomorrow, never do...and then something happens?

And just for the record, I don't eat bugs, grass or leaves. I'm not one of those adventure junkies you see on TV who end up in the middle of nowhere eating bugs, grass, or leaves. Why not? Because I prepare ahead of time and with foresight. I know this book will aid you in building a dependable bug-out bag but sincerely hope that you never have to use it.

TYPE OF BAG

So what type of bag do I suggest? Definitely not the cheapest you can find. Here are some items that I look for when selecting mine or when I'm helping someone else build theirs.

First off, you need a backpack-style bag. Don't get some single strap shoulder bag, no matter what size. Why? If you need your bag, chances are you're going to be moving around a lot, doing some walking. You'll need better weight distribution and back support. Two shoulder straps will feel much better at the end of a hard day walking through a rubble pile than constantly shifting from one shoulder to the other all day. Try carrying 15-20 pounds in a shoulder bag for most of a day, then, the following day use the backpack. How sore are you after that first day, and how much better do you feel in comparison at the end of the second?

Single strap shoulder bags, often called courier bags or "man purses," do have a purpose. They are great for the urban environment until you can get back to your bug-out bag. I carry my urban kit or get-home bag every day; it's just the basics to get me home. I'll cover this later in the book.

Now that we've decided on a backpack, you need to look for those that have a large main pocket. Remember, 72 hours. That's food and water for three days, not to mention if you have anyone else to look after. Backpacking bags are great, and large backpacks will do very well also—

but whatever you pack you have to haul. Just about every decent backpacking/hiker's pack have great padding on the shoulder straps and back support, but these aren't always quickly maneuverable. Large backpacks usually have good padded shoulder straps and decent back support but are much easier to manage.

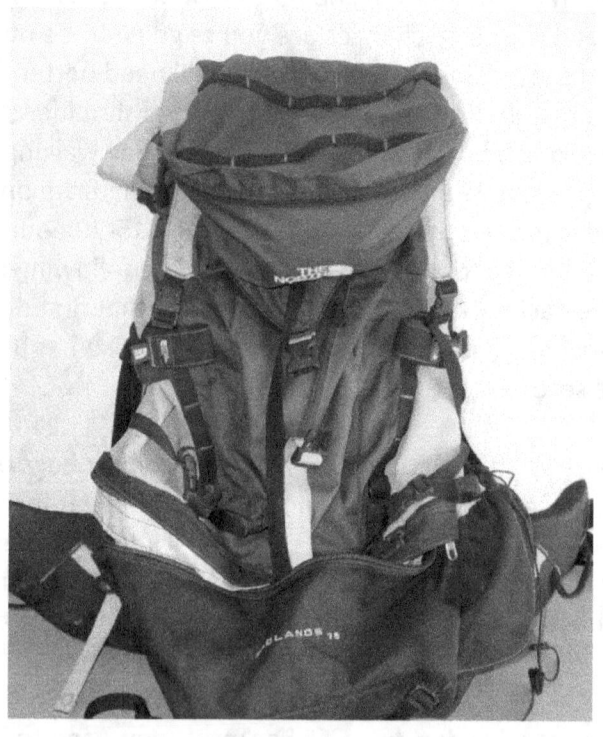

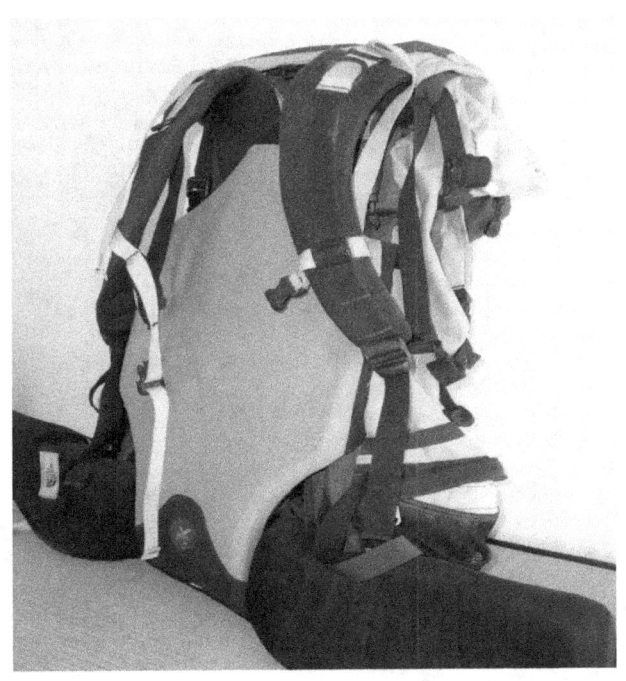

Personally, I use a MOLLE-type backpack. By itself, there are only three pockets, but because of the MOLLE system, I can add as many pouches, clips and straps as I want. I would recommend if you don't get a MOLLE-type pack, that you do at least get one with several pockets. One warning with using a MOLLE pack: it looks tactical, which draws attention because people associate anything that looks tactical with preparation.

Each pocket in your bag can serve a specific function, and with that, you can more easily remember where you packed items. A backpack that you find at an outdoor store should be more than sufficient; don't use a "school"-type backpack unless it's for a child. These are often cheaply manufactured, and so their stitching is very poor. A backpack with lots of straps or MOLLE webbing can be very beneficial when tying items down.

Look for bags/packs that have water-resistant material, whether it's the outside material or the interior lining. If you're ever in a situation where you have to use your bag, you need to protect everything in there. It may or may not be raining where you are, but where you are going it could be, and there's always something leaking somewhere. Maybe there's a busted water pipe that is showering water across the entire street that you can't go around, or the shelter's roof was damaged during the storm and is leaking over your cot, etc. Think ahead.

Hip straps are a bonus. They keep the bottom of your pack close to you. If you're moving fast, it'll keep the pack from slapping your back repeatedly with all that weight. Regardless of hip or shoulder straps, be sure to properly adjust them before you pack all of your gear. You may have to do some more adjustment after the pack is loaded down, but getting the majority of it done before hand makes it easier.

Also, look for double-stitched seams on the main body of the pack and the shoulder straps. Why? Think about the weight you are carrying. Do you really want to buy a cheap backpack only to have it burst apart when you need it most? Of course not, so inspect your potential pack for that possibility. Ripstop material is a bonus to look for in a bag, since it resists the advancing of any tears or cuts.

WHAT TO PUT IN IT?

PAPERWORK

Think about these different scenarios:

1) A tornado striking your house is imminent, and you take shelter in the bathroom located in the middle of your house. After the noise and shaking stops, you climb out and look around—your bedroom is gone. In your bedroom was the title to your car, your checkbook, and your wallet or purse.
2) A wildfire is rapidly approaching your home. Emergency responders have begun evacuating your neighborhood because the fire is moving so fast it can't be stopped. You grab what you can hold and leave in your vehicle. Your house burns down, and everything inside is reduced to ashes.
3) A radio emergency alert broadcast informs you that the river basin you live in is flooding rapidly due to rain upriver. Looking out the window in your home, you see a building floating past. Your house starts to creak. You run outside for a better look, just as your house is slammed with a rush of water and leaves the foundation.

While all are extreme circumstances, all are extremely possible.

What about your important documents? Your driver's license, social security card, passport, titles, deeds, savings bonds, etc? What if all those were lost in a single storm? So here's my advice: keep a waterproof document envelope with your paperwork inside. If you have a safe, that's probably the best place to store this information, but keep your bag close so you can transfer with ease. Also, make sure the envelope is waterproof as well—don't take any chances. If you don't want to spend $4-10 on one, use a gallon-sized freezer storage bag (but only one with a zipper to ensure a good seal). In addition to original paper copies, scan your documents and store the photo/pdf files on a waterproof USB thumb drive. That way, you have a contingency plan if your paper copies get wet and ruin.

FOOD

Let's talk about food. On a daily basis, a person needs an average of 2,000 calories. Now, depending on your size and normal physical activity, you may require more or less. There are a variety of free online calculators if you'd like to see what you need to maintain your current weight. When you are performing manual labor, you are burning calories, so it's very important to keep that count up. I'm going to list just a few items I carry or have used in the past.

Meals, Ready-to-Eat (MREs)...y*um*. For those of you unfamiliar with what MREs are, you're in for a treat. Basically, an MRE is a prepackaged meal sealed in an airtight polymer bag. These are prevalent in use with the military and government response agencies. The typical MRE package is rated from 1200 to 1250 calories. They come in a variety of entrée assortments: breakfast and lunch/supper meals, depending on the manufacture and type. I am very familiar with the military-grade-issue MREs and actually like them. On the other hand, some people hate the flavor, so to each their own. If I'm starving and you hand me an MRE, it will be eaten and not handed back. There are numerous companies that offer these meals.

Be aware, however, that some meals come with and without heaters. The heaters are activated by water and can heat your main entrée. Nothing worse than eating cold spaghetti or chili (so even if you may not need or use the heater, keep it for later). You never know. I personally carry one MRE per day, so that's three days' worth (3600 calories), not including the remaining 2400 calories I get from my other foods.

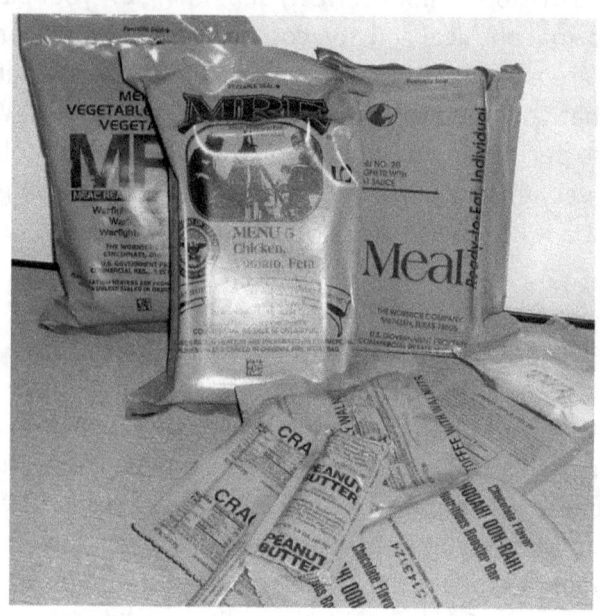

Dehydrated foods—like what you'd take backpacking or hiking—are excellent as well. These foods have had the moisture and oxygen removed so they can be stored long-term. To eat these foods, you will have to add boiling or near-boiling water to them. Once water is poured into the container, you will need to wait so that the water can be absorbed into the food. You can buy 72 food kits with these or individual meals. Depending on the foods you purchase, the calorie totals will vary. I've used both the breakfast and dinner meals. No complaints here, but it's not like what Mom makes. Just remember that for these, you have to have a reliable heat source to boil water, such as a small, portable camper's propane stove or a campfire. I like using a MilSpec canteen cup for boiling my water.

Snacks like trail mix, power bars, and granola bars are great sources for vitamins and sugar. The trail mix can come in economy-sized bags or personal-use bags. I prefer personal-use size because, if you share, then someone else's hand is reaching in your bag, and there's no telling what they've touched or when the last time they washed their hands was. In a harsh environment, the last thing you want to do is get sick with a stomach virus or diarrhea. Personal-use or single-serving packages will also keep you from overeating your limited resources.

For whatever food you decide to go with, I would advise a few things. Try the food out before stockpiling only what you want. If the food comes in a bulky package, break it down and get rid of what isn't a necessity. Make sure you have some type of eating utensils; eating spaghetti with dirty, nasty hands won't be a delight. Depending on the food you get, also make sure you have the appropriate cookware. Most MREs come with spoons, but this is not always the case with the dehydrated meals.

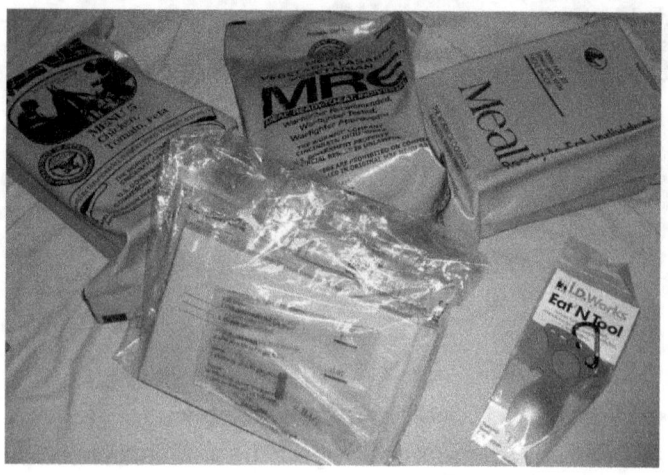

And finally, check the expiration and inspection dates. Past expiration, you're pushing it. Past one year after the inspection date on a box of MREs, check to see if it's still a viable food source by looking at the individual packages. The best website for information pertaining to MREs I've found that I personally use is www.mreinfo.com. This website can give you the breakdown of date manufacturing for a variety of brands.

WATER

You can "survive" for almost two weeks without food, but no more than 3 days without water. Water is the crucial element that sustains life; without it, dehydration will set in and eventually cause a less-than-desirable outcome. So in short, make sure you have water.

I want to mention containers and viable water sources first. So if you have a good sturdy water bottle (e.g Nalgene) or a hydration bladder bag, using tap water can quickly beef up your supply. A rule of thumb I've heard fairly often is two quarts of water per person per day with minimal activity and at least 1 gallon of water per person per day with heavy activity. The more you work, the more you will sweat and thus lose water. It doesn't matter if it's summer or winter, you will sweat when performing hard manual labor. So based on your expected activity, collect water accordingly.

I'm going to chase a rabbit for a minute here. Don't depend on the water in the faucet to be an endless supply. I keep three 1-gallon jugs of water in my pantry for just in case. Every few months, I'll buy new ones and use the old. That way, I know I've got water no matter what.

Filtration systems have made some major improvements over the past few years. Some of these are built into water bottles and others act like pumps. The recommendations that I would make to you are as follows: One, find one that is compact and light weight. You may have to carry this for the duration. Two, pick one that can filter vast quantities of water. Don't get a one- or five-time-use filter. You don't know how long you might have to use this. If replacement filters are available, then get some. Three, electronics are great, but they need a reliable source of power, and batteries are heavy. If you choose to use a battery-powered filtration system, carry your own batteries. The stores can be emptied out in a short amount of time or may no longer even be there.

Sanitizing light kits are really popular, especially the ones claiming up to 8,000 treatments. Using UV lamps, these kits will kill waterborne microbes. Follow the manufacturer's recommendations to sanitize the water in your bottle. An estimate of time would be about 90 seconds for a treatment, but again, follow the instructions provided with the equipment you purchase. Remember, these require batteries to work.

There are also purification tablets, which vary in size and what they can treat. Again, follow the manufacturer's instructions when treating your water. Basically, drop a tablet into your water bottle and wait a short time. Several people have "commented" about the taste of the water after using these tablets, but if you are using any water not flowing out of a faucet, how do you expect it to taste? This would apply to all water filtration, sanitization, and purification methods.

CLOTHING

Some might think this is an unimportant topic—that it isn't bare necessity—but just follow along here. What will happen when a cold front rapidly moves in or a severe thunderstorm strikes? What happens if you end up wading through a flooded bar ditch or street, getting soaked in not only water, but water with chemicals and maybe even waste? What happens if you are on your way to Grandma's for Christmas and get stuck in a winter storm, but because you were driving with a heater, you have on sandals, shorts, and a t-shirt?

I repack my bag twice a year, solely for seasonal clothes. Why? To have appropriate clothing for the upcoming seasons. In the cooler seasons, I like to have thicker socks (preferably wool), a beanie (double-lined is best for wind), winter gloves, a fleece jacket, a shemagh and a bandana, a small fleece blanket, and even a few packages of hand warmers. During the warmer months, I like to have a broad-brim hat (boonie style), multiple bandanas, and a shemagh. Things I always carry regardless of time of year are: spare underwear, socks, a long-sleeve cotton shirt, a light windbreaker, cheap sandals, washrags, and thin athletic shorts.

If you wear anything other than closed-toed shoes, you should probably throw in an old pair of shoes just in case you get caught in sandals or high heels. Can you imagine hiking through rubble in those? I do recommend flip-flops because there's a chance you'll have to use public showers at a shelter, campsite, or elsewhere. Fungus and other people's filth don't mix well with your feet. No matter how clean the area looks, wear them. Your feet get you going where you need to be—take care of them.

A long-sleeve shirt serves multiple purposes: it keeps you warm during the cooler seasons by providing insulation, and it provides a barrier from the sun and collects perspiration to keep you cool during the warm seasons. While great for normal everyday use, I don't recommend moisture-wicking athletic clothing for several reasons. First of all, your perspiration keeps you cool during hot days by helping to regulate your body temperature. Additionally, have you ever seen someone get too close to a campfire or stove with synthetic material on? The end result is, well, not pleasant. Cotton does not stick to you and burn your skin like synthetic material will. There are some Nomex (fire resistant) variations, but you might want something semi-rugged in case you have to hike or pass through any type of vegetation. Vine species or something like Catclaw Acacia will shred synthetic material in no time at all. Although, wet cotton *can* cause you to chafe if you have to walk a lot. There really is no perfect fabric to suit every hypothetical scenario.

LIGHTING

Of all the types of lighting products on the market, there are probably two that I would highly recommend using. But of course, I'll list some others that I have used as well. The first item that I heavily recommend is a headlamp with a tilt feature and an adjustable strap. Headlamps reduce the strain of carrying a flashlight; the light illuminates what you are looking at based on the position of your head and is very lightweight. Depending on the brand you pick, the battery requirements may also vary. Typically, headlamps will use AA or AAA batteries, so you'll have to make the decision on what additional batteries you want to carry. Making it so that everything in your pack requires the same battery type can be very beneficial.

My personal and work headlamps are both AAA powered. The batteries are light and only require two to three at a time. I would strongly suggest you try some out before you actually buy. I spent sixty dollars on a name brand a year ago, only to purchase a fifteen-dollar one about a month later...The cheaper headlamp is so much brighter and offers more features, like three settings of strength to choose from: dim, bright, and a red light. The dim setting will allow your battery life to last longer; bright will really give you great vision; and the red light lets you read easier—which would be good if you have to consult a map—and retain most of your night vision.

I am not telling you to go buy cheap, just giving my experience. I should have known to try them out before buying, so go find a store with demos and see what you like. There are some higher-priced headlamps out there that can put your vehicle's headlights to shame.

The second item that I heavily recommend for your bug-out bag is a solar-powered water bottle cap. Guess what? Solar power is free, it doesn't weigh anything, and it will be a constant (until it burns out, that is). The particular model that I have charges during the day and won't turn on, even with the switch turned on, if the photo cell detects any light. It's great! That means guaranteed light at night without batteries! There are some regular flashlights that do this too, but you have to remember to strap them to the outside of your pack. Most backpacks come with side pockets specifically for water bottles.

photo © sollight.com

Some other options out there are, of course, the classic battery-powered flashlight, the shake flashlight, the crank flashlight, light sticks, and strobe lights. Shake flashlights are flashlights that don't use batteries. Inside the body (typically clear) of the flashlight is a magnet that, when shaken, slides through a wound copper coil that charges a capacitor. These are great if you don't want batteries. However, the life of the light provided depends on the amount you shake. See the manufacturer's instructions regarding specifics of life expectancy.

Crank flashlights are basically the same concept as above, except you use a handle and crank it in a circular motion to charge the internal battery. There are some neat combinations out there that also include FM/AM/NOAA weather radios and might also have a small solar panel for charge during the day. Talk about efficiency.

Light sticks are small polyethylene tubes filled with a chemiluminescent substance that, when activated, create light for six to twelve hours in a variety of colors. The tubes are durable, and you can bend them easily without rupturing the housing. The chemicals inside are non-toxic and non-flammable, but read the product's labeling to confirm. Personally, I think these illuminate great at closer distances and work well for markers, such as on a fence post or highway sign, etc. Most of the ones I've used will float if need be; I've used one on a fishing line to illuminate the bait. There is typically a little tab with a hole in it toward the top of each light stick to allow the user to pull string or other items through to attach to whatever you want.

Strobe lights are lights that flash based on a chosen sequence. Typically, these are to alert people where other people or man-made features are located. Bicyclists use these at night, as well as firefighters, divers, and aircraft. They come in a variety of colors; personally, I like red because, again, it doesn't ruin your night vision as badly as white light does. Strobe lights are very inexpensive and will run on a couple of batteries for a good while. Consider them a good investment in case you ever find yourself in a situation where you're hoarse from yelling and have no water. Strobe lights require less effort to try to notify whomever.

TOOLS

Mankind invented tools to make daily life easier. Work smarter, not harder. There are so many different brands available, and prices will vary depending on the quality you want. When selecting some of these recommended items, think ahead about which ones can serve multiple roles, which can help to minimize the weight you'll have to carry.

A multi-tool can be one of your best friends in any situation. Typically, this tool includes a pair of pliers, a knife, Phillips and flathead screwdrivers, a can opener, a saw blade, and scissors. The brand and the size will determine what accessories your tool will be equipped with. One heavily recommended feature I urge you to look for is a carrying case that will allow quick access. I carry a couple of sizes, but even the small ones work great.

When you may be faced with cutting thin materials (making tender for fire, etc.), a good full-size sharp knife will be a blessing. There are two general types: fixed or folding. Folding knives are great for putting in pockets, but a fixed blade is usually a lot more durable. Most survival experts recommend a full tang fixed blade knife, which can be used to split items in two by hammering on its backside with wood, with minimal damage to the knife. I carry both, a folding for protection (concealed) and a fixed for "normal" tasks. A knife sharpener would also be a great addition. Some knives come with one, but the majority do not. Find one that's light weight, that's fairly small to pack, and that does not require oil to use.

Some items that can be very beneficial in numerous situations are ones that you can use to secure needed supplies, shelter, traps, or alarms. Acquire multiple sizes of zip ties, which have unlimited uses. Carabiners can secure items to your pack or be used as pulleys when tying down items. Bungee cords of various sizes can also help with securing items to your pack or shelter. They are typically lightweight and return to their normal form after use.

Tape—in particular "100 mph tape" or what is described as the super sticky gray tape—will aid in patching, securing, sealing, and many other functions. However, I would not recommend putting an entire roll in your pack. Two methods I would recommend are: 1) unrolling the tape from its original roll and then folding what you have unrolled with the sticky side inward, or 2) taking a #2 pencil and rolling the tape around the pencil with the sticky side inward. While you will probably not want to take the entire roll with you, a fair amount can be obtained this way.

If your multi-tool doesn't have a can opener, make sure you get one. Typically, food given out in emergencies is prepackaged to pull apart with the hands, but canned goods always make an appearance from those donating to the cause. I would hate to have food that I couldn't get to for days because there is no can opener to be found.

Flagging or surveyor's tape can serve many functions. Usually, it is found in high-visibility colors that attract the eye's attention. Individual rolls are very light in weight and can be easily torn. This tape can also be used to secure items, but normally not those of heavier weight.

Needle and thread are often overlooked items that can have huge benefits. They can be used for stitching of clothing or bags, and even skin in medical situations if no other means are available. If you frequent hotels, often some of the complimentary items will be a needle and thread kit which will work out great for your pack.

SHELTER

So if this were a long-duration preparation, I would recommend a backpacker's lightweight tent. A sturdy and durable tent that would actually be able to house you comfortably and keep you dry is worth spending the money for. Some might argue that it's extra, unneeded weight and that other items would work by securing to vertical arrangements. I would argue that, during catastrophic disasters, buildings, poles, trees, fences, and other vertical structures are destroyed or severely damaged. One advisement to using tents: choose the correct type for the particular time of year. Summertime tents that have large ventilation areas will only allow that cold air to swoosh through during the winter months. Some three-season tents have a rainfly that can be set up without the actual tent for a "minimalist" atmosphere.

However, since most disasters are short duration and you want to pack light, I would look at a rain poncho, a tarp, and an emergency tent. Rain ponchos are inexpensive and made of lightweight material. But remember, you get what you pay for. The 99 cent ponchos are great on your pocket book; however, they are mostly one-time use and will rip very easily. If you want to be found or noticed, find a high-visibility color. The thicker the material, the more durable it should be. Be cognizant of the vegetation in your area if it will poke or tear your poncho as your walk through it.

Look at a tarp that is fairly manageable in size. Some come in single and double layers. I prefer the double-layered myself; I feel it better protects from the wind and will have more strength to hold up if water were to collect in large amounts on it. I've gone backpacking before and only used my tarp for shelter. It will work very well, given that you take the time to set it up properly.

Another beneficial shelter is an emergency tent, but like it says in its name, it's for an *emergency*. These are made with a reflective material that helps hold in your body heat. However, emergency tents are very thin and very noisy. Basically, you will just crawl into this tent while it's on the ground. I keep one as a last resort and hope I never have to rely on it.

SAFETY

In the event that a catastrophic event does occur, whether it be large-scale or localized, there's a good possibility that medical personnel will either be personally affected and/or responding but unavailable to you. So let's go over some basic medical items. First aid kits come in a variety of sizes and assortments. Pick one that will last at least a few days if you have to replace bandages daily. Personally, I carry two kits: one is a one-person, three-day kit, and the other is a three-day, two-person kit. The logic behind having two kits is that if someone needs minor medical attention, I can use one of my kits without exhausting all of my resources. If your kit has any type of solutions or pills, be sure to keep them out of the heat and to check the expiration dates. Additionally, I carry trauma dressing ("battle dressing") and fabric tourniquets, mainly because if houses are lying over, smashed to pieces, there's a good chance that myself or someone in close proximity could be injured from the debris.

I once made the mistake of keeping saline solution in my bag, locked in my vehicle during a hot Texas summer. The bottle burst and soaked everything. Latex or the non-latex (neoprene, polyvinyl chloride, or nitrile) gloves are great to have for providing a barrier from fluids and for initially providing a sterile contact to someone or something else. Remember, however, that some people can or do have allergic reactions to latex.

Make sure all your prescription medications are filled and available for immediate use if necessary. Vitamins, aspirin, ibuprofen, or energy packs would also be to your advantage.

Three other items that I would heavily encourage for safety are a signal mirror, a whistle, and an emergency space blanket. All three of these items are extremely lightweight and can greatly aid in your survival. A mirror can be used to visually sign or communicate with someone. The whistle can blast high-pitched sounds with minimal effort to alert others. Your throat may be too dry to speak, but with this, all you have to do is blow air. If you don't have appropriate clothing, shelter, or sleeping gear, an emergency blanket can be a backup. By design, emergency blankets reflect body heat to help warm you, but be advised that it will not be as warm as a good sleeping bag or fire. It is an "emergency" blanket, so don't count on it as a primary resource.

Lastly, some items that can be a benefit but not a necessity are binoculars, a pocket thermometer, and clear safety glasses. Binoculars will greatly aid in the "surveying of the land" and gaining that situational awareness. Small, compact, and lightweight binoculars typically pack easier and require less room. A pocket thermometer, while it seems funny or excessive, can serve two main purposes. One is to measure the ambient air temperature; you may feel it's cold outside but not realize just exactly how cold it is. Knowing the actual temperature could prompt you to be more proactive in making and sustaining a fire or securing better shelter. Secondly, once sanitized, a thermometer can be used to measure a person's temperature. Body temperature regulation is very important; this could help measure whether a person is sick or suffering from a heat injury.

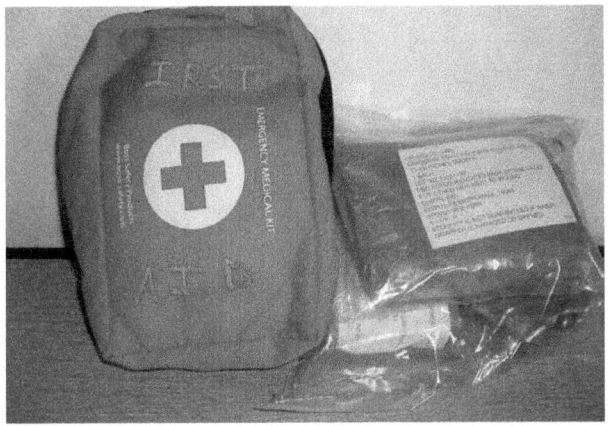

NAVIGATION

Ever heard that question "Where are we"? Depending on where and when a catastrophe happens, your pre-packed bug-out bag could greatly benefit you. Most people have gone digital with smart phones, using cell towers to navigate. Here's the problem: cell towers very quickly become overloaded during emergencies, if they aren't destroyed during the event. So what's your back up to navigate?

The first basic navigation tool is a calm head. Until something alters Earth's axis or orbiting rotation, the sun will rise in the east and set in the west. Although, depending on the terrain and vegetation that is present in your location, you may have a hard time placing the sun's location until it's closer to midday and the sun's overhead. If you can't see a clear horizon, watch for the dark and lighter parts of the sky. This can at least narrow down a generalized direction of east and west.

A pocket "mini" compass is the next basic navigation device. Depending on the size, one could fit on your watch band, the straps on your pack, or a separate bracelet specifically for that. I keep mine loose in a top pocket of my pack where I can easily get to it. Most of these smaller pocket "mini" compasses typically have the cardinal directions and notches in between without degree markings. A "regular" compass is larger but still fits in your pocket easily. The benefit to these bigger-style compasses is that they can be used in conjunction with maps. They come in a variety of colors and clear bases and have cardinal directions, degrees, and a magnetic needle. Some have map scales and aiming, or "gun sights." It is important to learn basic navigation skills with a compass; learning to triangulate your position will not only let you know where you are, but also allow you to find other people and vice versa given the correct azimuths and/or back azimuths from locations or features. The regular compass I use is actually one that will float, should it fall out of my pocket into any liquid. A quick tip is to make sure one end of some string is tied to the compass and the other end to your shirt/pack, or wear it as a necklace.

Maps are a great tool as long as you know how to read them (which isn't that hard). My recommendations are to get a state, regional, local city, and local topographic (topo) maps. Why? You can see what roads lead where and which direction features are. Topo maps show terrain, closest cities or towns, and some man-made features. It is very important that you learn the particular scales on the maps because each one can be different. This can affect estimating your distance to a feature or object. Some maps come in paper, plastic, laminated, or even digital forms.

Global Positioning Systems (GPS) have become very widely used in our lives today. They can be a great tool but also a detriment. Maps can be uploaded, routes mapped and saved, and have tracking, pinpointing, and even avoidance features. However, GPS units require a steady power source, and navigational GPS units can't tell you what roads are blocked or what bridges are destroyed and can potentially take you a longer route. Ones that require plug-in recharge may be difficult to maintain. Units that need batteries may be more easily powered by finding batteries or by using rechargeable batteries and a solar charging kit.

FIRE

Fire is a comfort feature—it will cook food, warm the body, provide defense, and light the dark. Be cautious of what you light and where you light it. Some materials contain harmful chemicals that can cause immediate health problems. Lighting a torch or campfire near flammable fluids, nylon, plastic materials, or extremely dry vegetation, etc. can result in a bad day for everyone.

Waterproof matches are great for all-weather conditions; however, depending on the quality, sometimes they can be hard to ignite. Make sure that you verify what specific surfaces the matches will light with; if you were to use regular matches that are not "strike anywhere," you can only use the box. A magnesium fire starter can also be a great tool, but be weary of the cheaper products. I found a mass-produced cheap magnesium bar (not made in the USA) and had the hardest time shaving off flakes. Even after making the recommended shaving pile size, the striker sparks would not light the pile. I spent about $15 on a second one and got ignition after the first try. Caution: the magnesium shavings will create a lot of heat when ignition begins. A regular "cigarette" lighter is also a great ignition tool, but be careful of the housing for the fuel. Cheap plastic ones will break very easily, spilling all the lighter fluid out or on you.

When starting a fire, it's important to have good, dry tinder in order to allow your fire to start, grow, and then ignite larger fuels. Some sporting good stores sell small, compressed particle-board squares that work fairly well and usually give a flame for several minutes. Cotton balls work well but only provide a short duration flame. I have added petroleum jelly to unrolled cotton balls, which adds a slightly longer burn time and more heat. Be cautious when handling, if you decide to use this method.

If you don't want to buy a starting fuel source, the best "free" one to use is dryer lint. Whether you own your own dryer or use a community coin-operated one, lint is abundant in every laundry load. Just collect and store in a moisture-free environment. Lint emits a smaller flame, but when mixed with grass or twigs, it will achieve the same goal. Adding petroleum jelly will also cause a more intense ignition.

Whenever you decide to make a fire, look at your surrounding environment. What fuels (which are anything that will burn) are available to you and are safe to burn? Is there dry grass you can collect to help build up your fire? Remember that after you are done with your fire, make sure to fully extinguish it. You don't have to use water, as it may be much needed. Use dirt, ash, or urine instead.

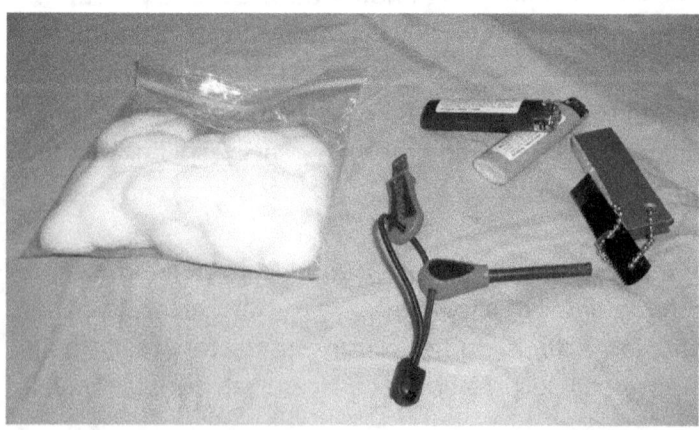

TOILETRIES

While some of the items mentioned in this unit may not necessarily be critical to survival, they will certainly aid in boosting morale, comfort, and hygiene. Hygiene is sometimes overlooked because it isn't part of the basic water, food, shelter, and fire categories. Regardless, I'm going to list some items that you should at least think about packing (but not necessarily all of them). Remember, weight is your enemy because it will tire you, and there's no telling how far your journey will go or last until help arrives...if it does.

I personally carry the following in my pack at a bare minimum; other items will sometimes be added or taken out depending on what I feel my needs might be at a particular time. Toilet paper—if there's nothing else in this section you pack, please at least take this. Unfortunately, there is only so long a person can hold in their waste, and when it's time, you may not make it very far to the next convenience store or residence. Disaster victims have at times used their clothing after going number two and even put those used garments back on because it's all they had. Don't be that person. Take the TP! Wet wipes (baby wipes) are great for not only "sponge baths" or back up toilet paper, but also to sterilize an area if medical treatment is needed.

Whether it's blistering hot or stingingly cold, some type of lip balm/protectant will greatly reduce your lips' exposure to Mother Nature. In addition to preventing chapped lips, the lip balm/protectant can act as a lubricant on some tools or other mechanical devices if you run out of the proper oil or grease to use.

A small mirror is great to check hard-to-see spots on your body, especially if you have any injuries. Hand sanitizer, which can be substituted by the wet wipes, is a quick way to clean your hands. If you think about what all you could touch or what someone else's hands have touched before they shake your hand...kind of gross. There are small travel bottles of hand sanitizer that work great and, depending on usage, can last about a week and a half. If you sweat, whether it's your feet or anywhere else, body powder will save the day. During Hurricanes Katrina and Ike, I used foot powder every day for the length of my assignments (14-21 days each). The humidity and friction between skin and socks will wreak havoc on your feet just from walking. Your feet keep you moving—take care of them.

The last of my bare minimum toiletry items are the absolute necessary medications. Ibuprofen and sinus medication are biggies for me, but you may require more serious medications. What you really need to think about is if your medication requires refrigeration. If so, you may need to seek out alternate medication types, leave earlier in advance of a known approaching disaster, or use cooling packs from the freezer until you can find a "permanent" cooling source. If you have to wear contacts, make sure you bring solution. There are often particulates in the air and scattered debris after a bad disaster. You will need to make sure if anything gets trapped beneath the contact lenses that you can wash it out.

Some creature comforts that you could consider are as follows: shampoo, the small travel bottles or the freebies from hotel rooms are generally a good size to minimize weight impact and volume; soap or body wash, again in the travel-sized containers; toothpaste and toothbrush for dental hygiene are a bonus, especially when you start making contact with others; deodorant, washcloth, and a lightweight towel will be great if you have bathing access. If all you can find is a water hose and no shelter, at least you have water to bathe.

Sunscreen will keep your skin from lighting up on fire after all day in the blistering sun. People have the common misconception that when it's cloudy they won't get sunburned. From personal experience, I can tell you that yes, you can, and it can be just as bad as direct sunlight.

Depending on the time of year and location, you may want some insect repellent. During Hurricane Katrina, I slept outside on a cot and swallowed mosquitoes every time I took a breath. With the exception of winter months, I will also carry repellant. Sleep is often impossible when you are constantly trying to swat away annoying pests that want nothing more than to bite you.

Sunglasses are very handy to reduce the strain on your eyes, even with snow. Don't rely on having an expensive pair that you may keep in your vehicle or home. What happens if it literally comes down to grab and run? Pack the cheapest sunglasses you can find that are comfortable. Lotion can definitely be extra weight but also a huge comfort. In conditions where your skin may dry out very quickly, such as winter or windy days, lotion will help keep your skin from cracking open and causing irritation, leaving you susceptible to infection.

Lastly, with all these "extra" items that you might possibly carry, don't forget to get a bivvy bag that can house everything so that it will stay organized and waterproof. A bivvy bag is nothing more than a small nylon bag with a drawstring to secure the items. Using these can help keep similar items together and make them easier to find when you need them. If you grow fond of periodically reassessing your bag, like I have, keeping things organized where you only have to pull out particular items will make it easier.

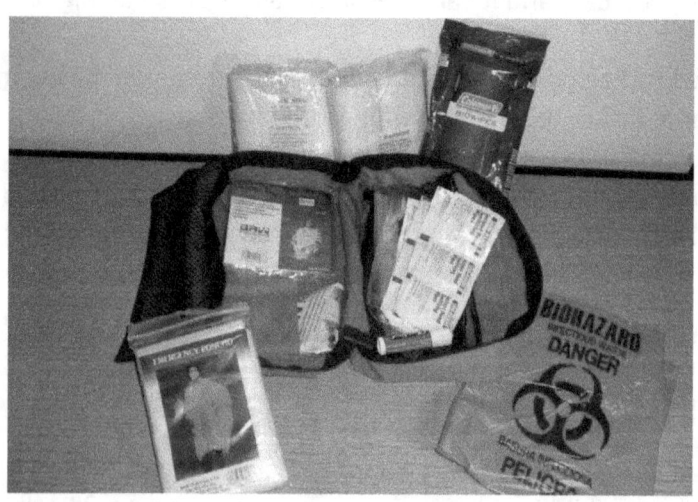

ELECTRONIC EQUIPMENT

The only electronic equipment I would recommend is what would be crucial to rescue or communication. If you have a cell phone, make sure you have a way to charge it. Having a household charger, a converter for a car, and/or a lightweight solar charger would greatly benefit you.

Some optional items that you may want are walkie-talkie radios, so that if you are with a group or another individual, you can maintain communication. Remember that radios will add weight, and so will abundant batteries needed to keep them working. Make sure they are the correct type of batteries before you load up if you choose to carry walkie-talkies.

Devices that make noise can attract attention, which is not always a good idea. Handheld music devices and portable gaming toys are great in normal everyday use, but in a disaster, they are extra weight and can give away your position if you may not want to be found by certain individuals or groups.

MISCELLANEOUS

There are little things often overlooked that can have a huge impact on your survival and recovery and on communications. A portable AM/FM radio, preferably with NOAA frequency ability, can be a wonderful asset. It will remain valuable if it can be recharged manually or by solar power. Some radios are accompanied with built-in flashlights and cell phone chargers that can connect with a USB cable. So instead of relying on batteries, you can operate the hand crank or place the radio where the small solar panel can receive sunlight.

Re-sealable waterproof bags are such a benefit and have numerous uses. Some uses (other than storage of items you want to keep dry) are as a retainer for water (that shouldn't leak unless punctured) or as a flotation device. I've personally used them to keep my gear dry during whitewater kayak trips. When I had an "unscheduled departure" from my kayak, the waterproof bags kept the kayak afloat until I was able to haul it to shore.

One item you will never find me without on a daily basis is paracord. Most respectable paracord is seven-strand braided and rated "550" for 550 pounds. Take that rating lightly because storage condition, age, exposure to sunlight, and exact materials used may affect actual performance. Typically, I only use paracord that meets minimum mil-spec requirements, but that's just a personal preference. I like darker paracord colors but will also pack white cordage for higher visibility.

Carry a good bandana or shemagh. Both can serve numerous functions, from keeping you cool to being used as a collection device or as a tourniquet. If you want to be seen, make sure to get high-visibility colors. Likewise, if you don't want to be seen, get dark colors or those that most directly reflect your local vegetation.

One item that is crucial to you and others can be a simple little pocket notebook. You can write down information you learn during your movement or you can leave a note for someone to find. Be sure to have multiple writing devices in case one should fail. I prefer a pen, mechanical pencil, and sharp-point marker.

"Cash is king," as they say. During most disasters, electricity is subject to be unreliable if the infrastructure is damaged. That means credit card machines and ATMs will not work if there isn't any power to run them. Have some cash available, but you don't necessarily have to keep it in the pack. If I was using my pack, I would divvy up my cash in multiple places on my person and pack in case I were to run into any deviants. Chances are good that that will happen. Look at every hurricane or disaster as of late that the US has encountered—somewhere, someone got mugged, robbed, or worse for their belongings. If you are faced with opposition, give them your "wallet" that only has a third of your cash. You still have more and are still alive.

Some other optional items that you may consider are: trash bags, rubber bands, disposable camera, fishing kit, freezer bags, clothing stuff sack, batteries, and cards. Trash bags can serve to collect trash, to provide shelter if cut at its seams, or to funnel rainwater into a sturdy container. Rubber bands are great for binding things down or to use as flexible restraints. A disposable camera would be beneficial in documenting any damage, especially if your cell phone no longer works.

Depending on what food sources you've packed and how bad the actual situation is, you may want a fishing kit that can serve to provide you food if near a non-contaminated water source. Freezer bags can serve as food, water, or even document storage if needed. If you want to keep dirty clothes separate from the remainder of your gear, perhaps you'd like a clothing stuff sack. This stuff sack can also be used as a pillow when filled up. If you use anything with batteries, you must make sure that you have enough of the right type. You may laugh, but cards or some other small non-electronic game will greatly benefit your mind by providing a calm distraction.

SLEEPING GEAR (*OPTIONAL*)

For sleeping gear, I would recommend backpacking-related items. Why? Typically they are lightweight, because weight does matter, and usually fairly durable for more than one use. Let's be honest though—not every product holds up to its name or is like the other one you bought.

Invest in a decent bedroll. Your back and body warmth may depend on the product you choose. I personally carry a backpacking, blow-up-style bedroll. Some of my friends prefer the polyethylene-foam-types that you roll up. It's totally up to personal preference. Just make sure if you get a blow-up bed roll that your lung capacity can support blowing it up without you passing out and that you have a good patch kit in case something punctures it.

Backpackers obviously are concerned with weight because of the distances that they may travel. If the weather is absolutely cold, you may need all the clothing you have to keep you warm, but what if you want head support at night? There are backpacking "collapsible" pillows that pack tightly into little bivvy bags until pulled free and then expand. They aren't the normal-size pillow but will elevate your head just enough to gain comfort and that familiarity.

If you choose to go as far as packing a sleeping bag, remember to select appropriately for that time of year. Summer sleeping bags will only cause you to freeze to death during the winter. Choose accordingly.

One other item I will briefly mention is a good hammock. As long as there are adequate trees to hold your weight, this might be an option for you. Remember, trees do break and fall over, so a tornado or hurricane could potentially wipe out trees over a widespread area.

KIDS (OPTIONAL)

If you have kids, they can be a great advantage. While wearing a backpack may be uncomfortable for long durations, the supplies they can carry will benefit everyone. Some food, water, and snacks might take a little weight off your pack or provide additional days' rations. A properly sized rain poncho and ball cap/full-brim hat would be well advised to keep them dry and shaded.

A change of proper attire for the season at hand and a small, non-electronic toy can greatly improve moral. You may need the batteries for the flashlight, so why waste them on a noise maker or an unproductive item that will only drain your supplies. Kids need to have something that will occupy their minds and keep them busy. Just something to think about—there's always a mental side to survival. Of course, giving them a "job" or task to accomplish will let them feel a sense of contribution to helping the family.

Load up the kids and make it a family activity to practice and repack everyone's bug-out bag.

INFANTS (*OPTIONAL*)

If you have infants, you must fend for them!

Remember these bare necessities: diapers (disposable or cloth), formula/milk, a bottle, wet wipes, a blanket, and spare clothes. Something to remember on the diapers: if one-time use diapers are soiled, you will need some type of disposal, and if cloth diapers are used, there must be a way to clean them before reuse.

Ensure the expiration dates on the formula are periodically checked and up to date. You will need to be able to keep the bottles clean by washing or boiling them. A blanket will not only provide warmth in the winter, but can also provide shade in the summer.

Plan on a way to carry your infant other than with your arms. After trekking for several miles, you may be exhausted and jeopardize safe carriage. There are many slings/wraps on the market for this purpose.

PETS (OPTIONAL)

Like infants, your pets will need you to fend for them. Be able to recognize what their food and water needs are for 72 hours. Most outdoor sporting good stores carry some type of pet supplies like containers, leashes, and other restraints.

Specialty backpacking stores typically carry items for dogs, such as "saddle bags" that balance over the dog's back so it can carry its own food and water, collapsible water and food bowls, and also waste bags. These stores also carry boots to protect the pads on dogs' feet; these could be a worthwhile investment if, in a catastrophic event, debris becomes scattered everywhere.

Take care of your pets. Don't leave them behind.

WEAPONS (LAST RESORT)

Do not interpret this section as me telling you to ignore any federal or state laws pertaining to any kind of weapon. The purpose of this section is only to get you to think about options. There could be a small local, regional, or even large-scale event, so how are you going to protect yourself or your family?

A good knife, like a full tang knife with solid grips that are not as susceptible to breaking or slipping when wet, would be greatly beneficial. Not only can you use this tool for setting up shelter and cleaning captured food, but also as personal defense. Don't think that just because you pack a knife you know how to use it defensively. Read up and even practice with professionals on self defense. The more you educate yourself, the less likely you are to become a defenseless victim. A machete is also a good tool to use not only for defense, but also for other constructive purposes, such as clearing a path or making a shelter.

Handguns are an option, if you can legally own one. Remember that most governments do not allow open carry and that there may be fines and jail time associated with breaking any laws. Carrying a handgun concealed with the appropriate and legal concealed handgun license (CHL) would be more beneficial by not advertising what you have. Oftentimes, a person may be targeted because of what can be visually seen. If you have a CHL and plan to carry, just make sure you practice effectively drawing your weapon with your gear on before you may actually have to. If you chose to use a handgun, make sure you actually know how to shoot it proficiently. Shooting it once, right after you bought it, does not mean that you are capable of firing it with precision and under pressure.

Rifles and shotguns are great for longer range, as long as you can legally own them. Unless you have a collapsible firearm or one that breaks apart to where it can be completely concealed, you might avoid carrying this openly (depending, of course, on the situation at hand). For a small event where maybe the power is out but there is no damage, walking around your neighborhood with bug-out bag and shotgun in hand probably isn't going to end well. Use your head. If zombies are in the streets, your country is under invasion, or the government has collapsed and is unable to restore order, then maybe you should grab one.

I am not advocating violence, only to know some options so that you can be able to protect yourself and those around you. Chaos has a tendency to bring out the worst in people—they revert back to the "survival" state. Look at Hurricane Katrina, when gangs were controlling neighborhoods and truckers were getting hijacked, and yet some neighborhoods banded together to defend their homes against those threats.

Remember, criminals don't obey the laws. They prey on the weak and defenseless. There may be no police, militia, National Guard, federal agents, or other government agencies to protect you initially, if at all.

CONCLUSION

Some last tips for building your bag: If you are carrying anything that needs to remain cool (like medicine or bottled water), insulate those items as best you can. Sometimes, wrapping a towel around a water bottle can keep it several degrees cooler than the current temperature, given time to adjust.

Read up or watch videos on how to tie simple knots. You would be amazed at how easy it actually is once you practice a few times. Knots can help reduce the amount of cord needed or make items more secure. Blue painter's tape or masking tape is great for short-term securing or binding of items, although high or low temperatures will greatly reduce the adhesive properties, so be aware.

You should now have a better understanding of the basics of building a bug-out bag. It's all about preference and what you are willing to carry, whether on your back or vehicle.

The best way to know if you built your pack right is to go camping with it. Give it a test and see where there is room for improvement. Be honest with yourself—more than likely, your first attempt will lack what are actually necessity items or will contain items that aren't up to par.

I mentioned at the beginning of the book an urban kit or "get home bag" and will briefly cover this now. Again, I use a sling-type bag that is lightweight, and I keep a 32 oz. water bottle, a small multi-tool, a compass, two six-foot strips of black paracord, a small flashlight, a headlamp, hand sanitizer, a small amount of cash, two power bars, a small first aid kit with medications, and a cell phone charger strategically placed. I check this kit frequently to memorize where every item is so that I can acquire something without even looking. It remains lightweight so that I can get home quicker when I'm around town. If I leave, my urban kit goes with me.

Don't feel obligated to purchase every item at once. Building a bug-out bag is a process, one piece at a time. Just don't take too long...you might need it.

CHECKLIST

	Weight	Pack #1	Pack #2	Pack #3	Pack #4	Pack #5	Total Amount
BAG							
PAPERWORK							
FOOD							
MRE w/ heater							
MRE w/o heater							
Trail Mix							
Power Bar							
Granola Bar							
Dehydrated Food							
Utensils							
Spoon							
Fork							
Knife							
Specialty							
Boiling pot/cup							
Cooking Stove							
WATER							
Purification tablets							
Iodine							
Light Kit							
Filtration Kit							
Nalgene Bottle							
Hydration Bladder							
FUEL							
Propane							
Butane							
Kerosene							

CLOTHING						
Underwear						
Socks						
Long-sleeved Shirt						
Footwear						
Flip-flops						
Beanie						
Fleece Jacket						
Windbreaker						
Hat						
Bandana						
LIGHT						
Headlamp						
Flashlight						
Light stick						
Strobe light						
TOOLS						
Multi-Tool						
Knife						
Zip ties						
Carabiners						
Multi-purpose tape						
Can Opener						
Bungee Cord						
Flagging Tape						
Knife Sharpener						
Needle & Thread						
SHELTER						
Rain Poncho						
Tarp						
Emergency Tent						
SAFETY						

First Aid Kit							
Signal Mirror							
Whistle							
Space blanket							
Trauma dressing							
Tourniquet							
Binoculars							
Medical gloves							
Thermometer							
Sunglasses							
Clear Safety Glasses							
NAVIGATION							
Button Compass							
Compass							
GPS							
City Map							
Region Map							
State Map							
Topo Map							
FIRE							
Waterproof Matches							
Fire Starter							
Tinder							
Cotton balls							
Dryer Lint							
Lighter							
TOILETRIES							
Shampoo							
Body Wash							
Toothbrush							
Toothpaste							
Shaving Cream							

Deodorant						
Toilet Paper						
Wet Wipes						
Washcloths						
Towels						
Sunscreen						
Lip balm						
Insect Repellent						
Small mirror						
Lotion						
Body Powder						
Hand Sanitizer						
Medication						
Stuff Sack						
ELECTRONIC						
Camera						
Cell Phone						
Cell Charger						
Power Inverter						
MISC						
Trash Bags						
Rubber Bands						
Disposable Camera						
Fishing Kit						
Paracord						
Sharpie Marker						
Cash						
Pocket Notebook						
Pen						
Pencil						
Ziploc Bags						
Stuff Sack						

Batteries							
Walkie Talkies							
Portable Radio							
Water Proof Bag							
Bandana							
Cards							
SLEEPING GEAR							
Tent							
Bed Roll							
Travel Pillow							
Personal Fan							
KIDS							
Small Toy							
INFANTS							
Diapers/Cloth							
Formula Milk							
Bottle							
Wipes							
Blanket							
Spare Clothes							
WEAPONS							
Knife							
Handgun							
Rifle							
Shotgun							
Other